# Anim
# Lions

by Nick Rebman

FOCUS
READERS

## www.focusreaders.com

Focus Readers is distributed by North Star Editions:
sales@northstareditions.com | 888-417-0195

Produced for Focus Readers by Red Line Editorial.

Photographs ©: MaggyMeyer/iStockphoto, cover, 1; RainervonBrandis/iStockphoto, 4; G Ribiere/Shutterstock Images, 7, 16 (top right), 16 (bottom right); KA Photography KEVM111/Shutterstock Images, 9, 16 (top left); ChandraDhas/iStockphoto, 11; jez_bennett/iStockphoto, 13, 16 (bottom left); Rob Hainer/Shutterstock Images, 15

**ISBN**
978-1-63517-851-7 (hardcover)
978-1-63517-952-1 (paperback)
978-1-64185-155-8 (ebook pdf)
978-1-64185-054-4 (hosted ebook)

**Library of Congress Control Number: 2018931100**

Printed in the United States of America
Mankato, MN
May, 2018

## About the Author

Nick Rebman enjoys reading, drawing, and traveling to places where he doesn't speak the language. He lives in Minnesota.

# Table of Contents

# Lions

Lions are big cats.

They can be brown.

They can be tan.

This lion has big **teeth**.

This lion has a **mane**.

A mane is hair on the head and neck.

teeth

mane

# Behavior

Lions live in groups.

The group has baby lions.

Baby lions are called **cubs**.

cub

Lions live in places
with grass.
Lions like to rest.
They rest under trees.

# Food

Lions **hunt** for food.

They eat other animals.

Lions are strong.

They can live for 12 years or more.

# Glossary

cubs

mane

hunt

teeth

# Index